The Poetry

by January Fieldz

Let's Fall in Love

Lets fall in love

Flowers in bloom

Lets fall in love

Spinning in my room

All that could be

Thinking of you

Hand in hand, we

Could it be true?

Summer delight

It's a hot rainy night

Every little plan

Sure, if you were my man

Lets fall in love

Lets fall in love

Flowers in bloom

Lets fall in love

I spin in my room

Dancing in the dark

Playful before bed

Walks in the park

All that could be said

It's a wonderful life

On the day I became your wife

If only it were true

I'd be not a quieter shade of blue

Memories spent

One little hint

Lets fall in love

Lets fall in love

It's a beautiful life

Lonely California

Tacos, sunshine and small dogs

Roses and palm trees

Huge mountains boulder the skyline

Surfing the cosmos

Missing Seattle and the friends I had

Gazing on real estate and big homes

Where is my sweetheart?

Walking in tennis shoe-d miles

Escaping the jailer for a slurpee

I wander California in absence now

of wine country, searching for home.

Long ago were laughs and dancing

in clubs 'til dawn

Replaced by waves of children

and wedding dresses.

Bouncing like a ball on the west coast

I fraternize with family

In the aftermath of madness

and the waking of a new life.

Book writing questions

and blank stares with no questions,

where is my sweetheart?

In this lonely California…

Sunshine Breezes

Sunshine morning breezes of orange blossoms,

and the houses of my neighbors

in blue, pink, beige, and white...

Planted well and flowering for hummingbirds,

Smiling with delight anew each day –

I sometimes kneel and bow to it.

It is so beautiful...

Everchanging mountains...

ocean mist every morning...

and at dusk...

the sunsets and the stars...

they are alive.

Maudlin Wind

Residue of every direction

slipping through my mind

tickling my teeth….

Squeezing the ribs of my morning

like a twister of hissing death…

Space questions answered

what are the answers now, for humankind?

Peace, Peace, Peace.

Light as air.

 Turning dollars in the wind,

gold nuggets and gold dust sifting through my spleen,

like a worm swimming through the aquarium of a changing body.

Gold dust, gold thoughts, sinking as a grave.

Rising as a spirit in Spring.

Reversing everything, or not.

Rose gardens and white gables.

Houses and haunts and everybody in between.

Skeleton closets and a new dress.

I have the hair of a gray ghost.

The pale face of Death.

 Utopian garden.

Be here now.

Be the rescue.

The hero.

Be the Win and the Winner.

For all of us.

Future Fire Plains

The southern snow covers my past tense existence
with the comfort of distant gazing.

Looking out onto the former attachments and
struggles I once thought made life so dear,

shivering in the hot California sun, I remember
from my January, how grateful feels.

For that which is new and brave, effortless to the
point of terror for its beauty and fragile for all its
glory.

I am the transcendent eggshell container of this
outrageous bravado we call True Love –

as tearable as a butterfly wing and as forward as
the summer bull,

unstoppable and wings to the fire, ready.

I welcome all that terrifies me newly in the face of
Love.

Black Rainbow

Wasted by the idle Porter

 the roadkill of souls in the afterlife

heave their misery in the face of a LSD breathing man machine

waiting in the shadows of the in-between like choking crawlers.

Shitting new sin into the face of old…

God immortal watches on with all that is Holy,

calling for courage and fire, astride

a caravan that is all but, comprehensive.

And the stars, the fire, the light and the love….

and all that carry the Holy spirit in their heart

have nothing left to do but, sharpen their arrows

and ensure sanctuary for the living.

Pink phospheresense lights towering

against a pale aqua November sky….

Dark purple clouds, drifting silently,

hanging lightly,

daintily with feeling.

Do they know that I love them?

Or just watch on, impartial?

Please know, that it is with passion that I everchange.

Alongside you for dear company so that you or I –

were n'ere alone.

Taj Mahal

Oh my Lord,

I call upon you to bless my mother, my family,

the very planet I walk upon…

Tears streaming, it is only You, to turn to. Who else?

Who else shall know of all things? In every dimension,

and planetary body? Who else to bless all things?

When all seems lost and broken?

There is only One Healer and One Hero ~

God the Good. Hater of evil, punisher of the wicked and…

Mender of everything.

In this Taj Mahal,

gold light filling every room,

every glance I take – is testimony to your tender
Love and care.

Never be far from me, Lord.

Live in my breast forever.

And when you see fit,

keep me to yours.

Holy Rose

The rose of Saint Anthony

sweet, the red of a sunset.

Resting in his palms,

taking in every tender petal….

the yellow center, as golden embers,

drops of sun from Heaven, caught in

the cup of beauty,

tender and fair,

as a priest's love for God.

Watching always, the Father,

the Son and the Holy Spirit and…

every Heavenly host, singing out

praises of creation, loving us.

I honor You, Father ~ Creator of All.

Creator of me, of he, of she and…

grower of all roses.

In the beautiful mystery of life,

the one of here and now,

built of rock and flesh,

and the everafter…

a terrine of Light and stardust!

One must never lose faith that our Father

and all who serve Him work

for our greatest good.

And our fair Mother holds us in her arms of night,

while every star sings jubilee!

And all these nights and days, sunrises and
sunsets ~

earthen palaces and ocean waves….

surge forward to be the,

rose in your hand,

the sunset in your eyes,

the Love in your heart,

and the very universe in which it all turns.

What more could you ask for?

A sign of love?

Gaze again, past the wounded

the fallen, the forgotten.

One who is wise and more loving,

holds us all in His palms.

For we are His tender petals,

fragrant and ever colorful.

And just as everything

we know was made by Him.

All that we do not was, also.

Have faith and when you have lost it,

find it again!

Fill you heart with Love at all costs,

and you will know God.

Stafford

Stafford, you were a goal, a prize to be won

A life under the lights amidst whirring rides and childrens' screams

We tossed balls to bring you home

Riding in my purse, you were on your way to your first home

I held you with your brother, Carmichael, in tenderness

Loving the beauty, the regal gold of royalty that prize goldfish are

the winning kind…. the kind that live fast, die young….

Your death is a failing in my eyes,

mine, fate, time, corporate structures of fish food, faulty water….

I mourn your death, as does, Carmichael…

we feel your loss and send you love, Stafford.

Your soul swims eternal in the palm of God's loving hand,

and you will never be forgotten.

I love you.

<u>Zoo 2000 und u…</u>

Drum circle and yellow leaves…..

The mighty oak stands in its splendor,

in shades of grey, and black, and harmony…

The zoo of a eastern wild wood…

dressed in bark and canons of Naval fire,

jungle music and singing voices,

echoing off of every trunk from which the hawks fly,

bouncing every voice which utter, from tree to tree.

Resonant echoes of childhood shrill at the chill of twilight….

Sitting with Dick on his porch, listening…..

smiling with friends, with King Georgian gentlemen,

on porches or downtown, until the night calls.

Driving past fields of hay and corn… for miles….

Past the mason cemetary and James Madison's offices,

Stirring with change, as the sun falls.

i feel like i should apologize for something
saying too much or for the way i left, too fast
i can feel the madness stirring… like tiny red ants
in my veins whirring, ready to run or bite or…. i
don't know
somehow i am whole and wise and yet there is
this one part of me i just can't control, screaming
to be let out
telling me it is time to go and the whirring of
words on the radio say "carpe diem, dollface."
and i can't waitican'tstandanotherminute,
imustimust!!!
oh, i know what you're thinking….
you are calling me crazy and asking around for
answers
but, some things defy definition and endear the
lack of reason like spontaneous combustion and
shooting stars, flash floods and anti-gravity in that
one little spot in California where grows the
Joshua tree… easy as pie, I tell no lies, but I run as
I please! across the country and through the desert
in the summer sun, to the ocean where I will meet
you with a kiss, if only to walk hand and hand for

an afternoon or arm and arm and sandy-legged upon the beach in knotted love, with thee, just you and me… as if it were a dream, the best dream I ever had…. the best hour, day, as long as it lasts…. forever, if it were up to me.

***

In a sudden fury again, wine coursing through every part of me that has been forgotten has been lost, has been tossed, has been besotten with the he's and the you's and the where with-alls of the whole damn mess that is supposed to be my existence as a woman.

I hate sounding dark but, there is that element that persists in broken promises and haunted dreams, screaming rage and now suddenly, it seems i was too slow to turn the page on my malcontent at being stuck in this body, stuck in this place where everything seems to move too slow and nothing makes sense.

Already ashamed of myself, for the way I slash at and around all of those beautiful things that I invite
all of the creations that i create from those visions of my sight that i mold into little villages from the clay….
smash! smash! you're dust again and I'm displeased with everyone

"Especially, you." the deserter the silencer... looking into the mirror. I see myself looking fatter and more haggard than ever before. Living more in my mind than in my body, body being such a chore... I run with a million ideas at once into far off distant country countries of promises I can keep to myself, of towns I can pass through...

Knowing i don't have to stay. Its just a contest, some new scenery.... the scorching madness doesn't have to stick, the loneliness and the loss.... it doesn't have to tick... tock.... off goes the bomb of my next dice toss...
I wish I could have loved you, I wish you could have loved me.... I wish I was a little lamb and silent as apple tree.

I wish I was, I wish I might... meet you on the street tonight. Under the yellow lamp on the dark street
where no one knows to be there but you and me where right on the dot, at 10 o'clock... we are standing there unembarrassed, bonded by a kind of understanding no else would understand.

I tend to go deep and you tend to go light and I sometimes do the craziest things, dangerous too....
smiling you like to laugh and i like to laugh along with you.... hey, what do you think about... nevermind, I'll just shut my mouth just as long as you kiss me...

Oh, kiss me… just kiss me… and everything will
stop spinning. kiss me, just kiss me and i'll be your
everything, your angel,
such a good good girl…

@#$%$#

mail me an escape
wrapped up in a pretty package
with stamps and pleasant wishes
to me, in a heat, peeling the keys
off my keyboard, beating the days
and the nights with sips of wine
and forbidden cigarettes
pocketed in the folds of New York City
fleeing for my life
fleeing from the winter
i sunk into the South
the place where i was born
and have not been in
such a long, long time….
and here i am… with big plans
bigger than the ones i had before
i left Seattle, escaping the fog
and sorrow of too much work
too much play and not enough rest
i watch the friends i had from afar
and some i miss and some i dismiss
cold and hot, what does it matter anymore?
some care and some do not, for all the right
reasons
were you seeking superficial gratification from
me?

perhaps it is why i left in the first place
play a game of wait and see
but, now its a new game
a new name….. a new take on an old memory…..
untangling, rearranging i keep on….
getting drawn back to where i really want to be.
except, i've a few things to prove
a few things to do,
who knows what will ever be?

NYC

heartbreaks like bottles of wine upon the stone
upon the rocky rocky road of my delusion
oh, you have made me such a fool
not even my lies or my disguises can elude
how very sorry i am.

pink delight in one smoggy city night after
another
thought i'd be on my way, thought i'd find some
other
love and life for me, some other someone to be….
but looking on the wreckage of all i left behind
i find that i feel sorry and i am longing….

in a hold. because i don't really want to come back
we both know now you've got nothing for me
though everything that meant something, i have
left behind
i can't seem to go forward, blinded, for some
reason,
a reason that i drown with bottle after bottle of
holy wine

can't see just how its all going to work out

the only thing i can confirm, is that the lights are
down
and my jeans are dirty, its past 12:30 and i no
longer care
about the people who see
about the people and the scorn and who talk shit
on me

because i can only think one thing
singular and so sincerely so so….
i think that you and me,
we still have some time to go
we still have some secrets to keep

some kisses and some well wishes
some riots and some quiet times….
some somethings….
for the fight has not quite left my core.
hope will avail us.

ahhh… but, wait.
here i go again.
down the wrong, wicked path….
back to where i am no longer wanted…
in the past, the broken past oh, i am still so
haunted….

((((+))))

do you know the times when you are thinking
this is it. this is the compression of moments
i've always dreamed about, the pressure that i lust
for
covered in make-up and fantasy
surrounded in chimes and rattle shaking
thoughts of love and creativity, kissing and
living. the epitome of life found in back seats,
found on scraps of paper written at bars and
backstage
saying, "you make me eternal. find me again one
day."
because its true… about you… touching me-
that's what love is all about.
no ifs buts or maybes… whens or thens… just is.
just is honey, just is. qualify and quantify it not.
you know what's happening out there.
the wars are crushing the populations into the
ground
the causes are drawing their broken bones all
together again and there is no more room for
broken people, lost children or selfish causes.
we are the Earth now, the force destined to save

we are the ones, drinking the wine and smoking
the weed those of us who are willing to lead, to
step forth
and herald the sound of the underground
for light has long been the underdog
long been the slow winner of things
hail, Love! the darkness will sink under
and those of us who are the lovers of life
the champions of the trees and the skinny dippers
in all the great rivers which we keep on keeping
clean
We shall be the ones celebrating our victories
these victories of which angels sing
these victories of which our hearts bring
in the shadows and out of the illusions
yea- this is the greatness that shall be.

%^&*H

drunk on Chianti halfway across the world from
you
but what would it matter?
if i was in you town?
you'd just be walking around pretending it don't
matter.
pretending things are fine and that you don't got
the time for me.
that's right. i know how it can be. sweating in the
city.
working the jobs that get things done and then at
night,
we spill our blood into the streets in search of
meaning
in search of being and coming and winning and
yeah….
i know what you mean when you say that you've
earned it,
you've won it, you've been there, you've gone the
length-
hey, guess what? the guy next to you on the bus
has been there too
not so different and not so distant from what
you've lived, from me or you.
can you see that we are all here together,
variations of the ONE LOVE like sparkling white
to dark port
we are the angels, the beings

that are moving and grooving across her fair face…….
do you see it? every tiny motion and feeling….. it matters.
it matters and makes the difference between what kind of life
you are living and what kind of love we are giving, sweethearts….
see it and be it. courage, my brothers and sisters. courage to love-
FEARLESS.

(((((((((IIIIIII)))))))))

sand, sea and wind ~ eyes wide open
visions of the open road
renewed as the desert in spring blooming with
sage
music in the night by campfires built in laughter
wild running through the woods where the owls
go "hoo hoo!'
where are you, my lover? i will find you, yet!
i imagine you singing to me and the sound of you
is warm
and makes me so…. unguarded… and tender and
new,
eager for magic making and promise exchanging,
knowing
i will never flee from you and you will never shy
from me
because we can clap our hands in time by the fire
where our friends are smiling and laughing
feeling the joy that unites, who has time for
fighting?
or tears? the years are little stitches in one big quilt
here, i am the calico patch to the left
and you are the paisley band to the right
see? there are only a few places we meet
before we turn off in different directions
riding the white space like a river to its end

so kiss me when you see me again and don't think
twice.
i said don't think twice!
i'll see you and you'll see me, strangers we
racing hearts and sweaty palms, eyes downcast
looking everywhere and just past but… here here,
my sweet!
look before i disappear…. i'm shy, too!
hand in hand we will walk in smiles for coffee
and three hours later in good conversation,
the world is a rainbow and everything tastes like
candy
(i like rose pastilles, by the way)
and we wander together, will you wander with
me?
across this beautiful country with our hearts wide
open
open as clear blue sky and big fields of green
there will be times spent in metropolis, too….
when i'll wear dresses and finger nail polish
and you'll probably go to bars and i'll throw
dinner parties
and even in the city, with the traffic and the
beggars…
we'll be happy. because i will never stop loving
you.
(you, who love me so much, too.)

Wine Festival

100 degrees in the shade today
barely past early Spring
the summer heat saturates
red cheeked and dirty feet
in white cotton and straw hats
to survive today's wine festival
purusing art and antiques,
fine jewlery and the treasures of hunt country,
the green and white tents were the only shade
on the lawn of St. John's on Saturday
mother of pearl place holders for poker played in
1852
the set cost her a mere $1,500 and some
astonishment
as the circle of women laughed, aghast at her
whimsy.
Admiring a painting nearby,
I gripped the handle of my box
envisioning the delights I'd attain later on
embibing the three bottles of delicate wine.
Sober, I dare not taste in this heat,
the threat of fainting, despite my sunhat
is clear enough, in the wobbles and white flashes.
The sun set in pastel rainbows
above misty fields of rolling green
elegant trees, fine as the finest ladies

held their limber arms in pose, dripping with
minty green
the long-horned cattle and horses seemed more
regal than usual
land of kings and queens, land of dreams, land of
my everything.
Soon the heat will be too much to bear,
and I'll be heading north- then perhaps I'll go
west…
But, the beauty of Virginia never fails
to knock me over with her nuances,
so fine and subtle, yet so strong in her Seasons,
this is the land of my heart,
the part of earth that i love best.

<u>Fuck Your Silence</u>

i tell you one thing you've got all wrong
thinking i'll just tag along as you string
one silence after another
you make these assumptions about me
perhaps you think i don't notice or care
but, let me tell you-
i notice every damn thing and care more than you
know
in your world of mock insignificance or
superiority
tell you what i'll do
when you refuse
to reply, thus denying respect to me
i'll cut you loose. just like that.
because i've jumped through too many hoops of
fire
too many tests and trials and though you think
i may have the world at my feet
and its some privileged luxury for you to deny the
common respect
you'd give to any stranger
i am telling you, you who become the close
minded bigot
racist, sexist, worse than Hitler in our modern era
when you assume things about me.
don't believe your eyes, or the lies you'd like to
see
underneath we are the same, you and i

and when you separate or remove
telling yourself that you're too good
or not good enough…..
you make yourself a fool.
for not everyone is cruel.
not everyone is cruel…..

<u>The Last Song of Sorrow</u>

By the lamplight do I write these words that seem
Unfamiliar yet so familiar, like a reincarnation of
the same old dream
Here, sleepily under starlight do I listen to the
black night sing
A perfect love song where nothing goes wrong,
unstained by memory
I ask why I bother, why I continue to ponder your
sweet smile
I know that the chances, suggestive glances can
only last for awhile
The months have past and my glass is full to the
brim with denial
Your kiss on my mind, I drink steady and aplenty
'til I'm soft as a child
Here come the visions. Come beauty, dance
through my head!
Can't bear to make more decisions, so I never
leave bed
Here's one glass for sorrow and two for where my
luck led
Still by tomorrow those letters from long ago, will
still be unread
What shall I do? Everso alone, here is nowhere
with no love of my own
I just keep wandering down these winding roads
Manhattan or Mississippi, I care not where I go

My lips forget how to smile with each mile, out here in the cold
Trying for a clean break, I've often tried to erase and replace you
I was broken inside so with each new handsome face, I tried hard to see it through...
The first time you broke my heart was only the start of the abuse
Because by the second and third, how absurd, my love remained steady and true
The clock is ticking, the snow is sticking and the days go by
Every new endeavor or remote pleasure feels like a lie
For try as I might, come day or night, I hear my own sad, soft sighs...
And I love you, yes I'll love you no matter how many times I tell you goodbye.

Fight Like Knives in Dark Alleys

fight like knives in a dark alley
slashing and trashing my life away
with wicked words and cold feelings
sentences that invalidate my being
existences made small… and insignificant.
mothers… fathers…. how they complicate
eradicate…. make one regret breath
make one rage against all the rest of life
when they are the children of your childhood
more like little sisters or brothers, foundlings you
watch out for
they somehow manage to put you in charge
old enough to walk, old enough to talk
my youth stolen.
i am the mediator, the cook, the counselor,
never the child, never the daughter
i am the authority from my first word
used as a shield, a battleground, a sounding
board, a mother and confidante
of secrets i should have never heard
i thrash back and forth from one extreme to
another
changing faces and names
never really finding myself
until i am all alone
because everyone is always trying to hang a sign
on me

and those that i love
always seem to find some reason to put them
selves above
so high above me....
so special, so rare, so….. full of shit.
and you wonder why i never stay long.

Unrest.

Impossibly hot, even with all the windows wide
open
I stay close to the fan in a gauzy nightgown with
no covers
the dog is panting on the floor
and the cats are restless, overly affectionate
for they know I do not sleep
turning in my bed, constant in my searching for
comfort in escape, any escape
I'll take whichever kind comes first
feeling limp and transparent,
muscles aching from the heat,
crying with eternal thirst
I cannot stop stirring, despite fatigue
now the cat's toy, pawed like a mouse
high up in the attic room among the trees
and outside the house hangs a nameless phantom
escaped from hell,
watching me in weighted silence, closing in like a
woolen blanket
aggravating the unrest I long to quell,
stifling every girlish dream I'd hoped to be having
of you….
my imagination wilted by neglect, now a ruined
bouquet
spoiled in the cruel afternoon,

shocked by the frost of your stoic display, of
absolutely nothing…
you give me no pleasure, nor cause to dream…
withholding the slightest sincerity,
the hammer falls of each passing day
marked all, by your bitter silence and the bruise it
leaves
how it crushes,
fruit of hope, fallen from yon forbidden tree…
deny my existence
until the art of my being has died
and the gift of exuberance becomes extinguished
dark as a moonless night
even the stars are hid by a humid haze
so somber is my heart
and thankless,
in the oven of my lonely days.

Wistful Winter Wanderer

By the lamplight do I write these words that seem
Unfamiliar yet so familiar, like a reincarnation of
the same old dream
Here, sleepily under starlight do I listen to the
black night sing
A cosmic love song, where nothing goes wrong
and remains unstained by memory.
I ask why I bother, why I persist to ponder the
charm of your smile
I know that the chances and suggestive glances,
only last for a while.
How the months have past and I've filled my glass
to the brim with denial
With you on my mind, I drink steady and aplenty
'til I'm soft as a child.
Here come the visions. Come beauty, dance
through my head!
Oh, I can't bear to make more decisions, so I never
leave bed…
Here's one glass for sorrow and two for where my
luck led…
and by tomorrow those letters will still be unsent
and unread.
Finally alone, here is nowhere with no love of my
own.

I just keep wandering, down these winding roads…
Manhattan or Mississippi, I care not where I go.
My lips forget, how to smile with each mile, forsaken and un-kissed, out here in the cold.
Making for a clean break, I've tried to erase and replace you
I was broken inside so with each handsome face, I tried hard to see it through…
But, the first time you broke my heart was only the start of the abuse.
Because by the second and third, isn't it absurd? My love stayed steady and true.
The clock is ticking, the snow is sticking and the days go by
Every new endeavor or remote pleasure feels like a lie
For try as I might, come day or come night, I hear my own sad, soft sighs…
I love you. Yes, I'll always love you- no matter how many times I say goodbye.

&&^%@#$%^&()

Acorns pouring down on me,

From up on high yonder tree,

In love, for being of One with me….

Oh Love, I love your company.

As Crowes Fly

Blue eyes soft as southern haze,

wrapping me from head to toe…

as summers do.

I watched you move from here,

to there –

one thing at a time,

one woman after another,

minding my own business.

Couldn't help but, notice

sewing my dresses

sewing magic into everything I do

praising God,

praising you.

I left off in my mind

skinny dipping where there was

no one I knew, well.

I swam in it for awhile

but, there are finer things in…. memory

when it comes to you…. future tenses

wondering what would happen

around the next corner, blind as all

blind as all….

I said, from a sunken corner,

brick patios and red wine, hot sun

crows fly, time sailing

lives are falling and in my own mind, I'm
supposed

to name every answer,

….'til we meet again….

Invincible

Overcome by secret agenda

a secular outlook

I battle the lower nature of others

in their stupidity and corruption

with my Higher Light and very life

throwing my heart out, like an old back

pissing wine and shitting blood

meeting the unknown with blessings against

a curse, going on through the night

like a warrior, like the Red Dragons of time

like the Griffon of my heart,

wielding Esmerelda, the blade of Ultimate Truth

cutting down Demons.

I survive by the day, in God's Love

wearing His armor, wearing Her dress,

a world of Love made to create in Love

to breathe and to speak in Love,

and though my Light draws the Shades,

of night in their ignorance, coveting all that I have

I defend and stand strong knowing

that in Light and in Love, I am invincible.

Smoking Lonely

Smoking lonely,

cigarettes past regret

the kind that went hoping

the kind that went creeping

around corners,

lost in the broken streets

of Detroit.

Cracked out on pipe dreams

the ghost of romance

black-faced by the tracks

knife blades and scar tissue,

I thought I knew you.

Believing, relieving in you,

stepping to the side,

I flew open wide and full,

of love, of hope, of pretty thoughts

dropped, into the silence

of a black theater

showing only film noir

silent and sad, smelling

of must and the might of one

viewer, myself….

the only patron in the theater of us….

whatever that was…

is… never to be…

never to be seen again.

Canopy

Lush rain sliding over my shoulder,
watching from a perch,
high above the canopy,
I roll my hip forward, lurching from a crouch…
crawling in the murky heat, towards you.

Close your eyes, Paul.
You will never see it coming.
I am your hunter and you, my prey.
I will find your weakness, biting down upon it,
I will savor every bite.

Tell me nothing, we'll do no talking.
Frozen for a time,
unlocking the grid.
I will find your breaking points
and take them into my mouth.

Will you kiss me? Will I sing for you?
Will we know the other,
when it is through?
Only monkeys know.
Or perhaps the macaw will tell?

One day… sipping on the sweet tea of your smile,
I'll sit with you like a quiet afghan,

wrapped around your lap, warming you all
over…
your hands threaded through me,
tangled together.
Everything I Have Is Yours
Everything I have is yours, you're a part of me
Everything I have is yours, my destiny
I would gladly give the sun to you
If the sun were only mine
I would gladly give this earth to you
And the stars that shine
Everything that I possess
I offer to you…
Let my dream of happiness, come true
I'd be happy just to spend my life waiting at your
beck and call
Everything I have is yours- my life, my all.

Low Vibe

My thoughts are moving like molasses.

Deep, dark, and slow.

I don't care what happens tonight.

Deep down in my chest I feel hollow.

 You wreck me with your little ways

of eating at my soul

Do I fight you, despite you, pacify you

or do I just fucking live in a hole?

 Anger. Sweet and fast rushes through my veins

Like sugar or heroine

Dark water, dark water

Wash me clean again.

Sincerely and truly I crave release

from the claws of your negativity

your bad energy and low vibes

exhaust me ceaselessly.

 Crawl away on your belly

see what the dirt is

You are choking me

Stain my aura no longer.

sdfsklfjaosiru38ur32

I wish that I could be air

lolling in dark corners

breathless, weightless, heartless

air blowing in, out of our house

air leaving the room without being noticed.

I am drifting away with new dreams of you,

sitting here, in the middle of a Virginian brooke

on a lawn chair, my feet wet and head

sky high thanks to a glass of wine and oh,

I never would have guessed

that you would have ever noticed me.

How much luckier can I be?

I've been writing letters lately,

you know, the paper kind, online….

and bidding on typewriters, colored pink

because I think, that the real world exists

in the touching of textures, the scents of affection

and some people are so scared of that.

But, you're not so one dimensional are you?

How about you go beyond two... how about 3?

How about you and me one day this summer,

quiet in our strangeness but, laughing in our sameness...

together on a blanket, wearing shorts and shades,

I can see it now. Know that I believe –

in picnic baskets and gorgeousness all the time.

And I suppose you may let me out of my

iron cage with your gentility and serenity,

...and I suppose I may fall

drastically in love with you.... if ever I

were to be by your side.... again someday.

Sweet Soma

Almighty, everliving, glorious, gracious One….

I breathe you in,

exhale you out,

praises for You on each breath.

You are the compassionate Mother,

a powerful and wise Father,

and I know you more intimately, every moment.

Thou hast cast me into fires and baptized me in holy water ~

in love, sweet ever-giving, everlasting Love.

You gave me two parents, opposites in nature ~

the delusions of Hell have been many,

but, you never gave up on me, leading me along the way.

I have come through to you at last, my only Reality.

My sweet Soma. All I know is You.

You are all there is.

I take each footstep, knowing you more and more.

Your beauty is everywhere and I am speechless,

for your Perfection leaves me in awe.

How could I have been so blind before?

Your Grace is upon me and I am on my knees giving thanks,

oh, Love… your power is all-conquering.

I am your hands and feet, Soma.

Great and glorious God, thy will be done.

I have passed through Hell's gates

and arrived on the other side of the doors of perception,

I see you clearly everywhere, I hear you, I receive you.

You are the only Mother and Father, that I know now~

The Truth, the Way, the Light.

Shin'ah

Space, sweet space

Void of creation

Beauty for which

every creature under the sun,

catches its breath.

Sweetly, gently…..

With the grace of

light dancing a ballet,

as a lover of love, itself.

Primary Feminine,

divulge your mysteries…

Your daughter waits at your feet,

smiling to you,

as if watching you put on

red lipstick for the first time

did you witness,

my lips move in unison with yours?

Unconscious of myself,

I was born to walk in your footsteps.

Sweet Mother,

I welcome you with love,

fresh and innocent as the very spirit of Spring!

Loving your power and your many charms,

for all of creation

begins

with

you.

Realized

The moon was dark and new when I REALIZED all …

I walked to the other side of myself and saw.

I stretch my arms and say, "AHHHHH….!"

Now I know… turning, looking….

..smiling with the miracle of,

such tender love, the journey I've just come from….

Before and after…. human and god….

masks of sacrifice and poetic embrace,

dark and light…

we sleepless expressions,

angles of light, split like prisms into our many colors

angels of beauty and terror –

Grinding against, like lovers))

cut with your whispers,

in the night of my illusion.

I am free.

I see at last.

Sweet, sweet love….

what a beautiful world we live in.

Realized in the stillness….

There are no limitations,

except that of perception.

RELEASE that which is false, with love!

Everything is energy…

God is everywhere… everywhere!

our Nature is of Ecstatic Joy and tremendous Love

reaching everywhere, everywhere!

through grasses and rivulets of water snaking through dry country

through giraffes in Africa and moles in West Virginia,

…and every song sung by every bird, man, or wolf!

through the bums stinking down on the square and through you and me!

through every living, breathing plant, animal, and creature,

…. even the moss!

We are so blessed….. we are, we are…

we are one blessed GREAT *cosmic* THING!

Blanket of light, fingers and eyes of God… shed your skin, small identity.

I saw you in the silence and cried for your sweet pains and yearnings….

what a distance, my Love.

My sweet sweet love…. nothing will ever be the same again.

(Love yourself, just for taking the journey.)

For here I am, as ever....

Beloved.... you are, we are.

So very loved...

(thou art, {{be-comingcuming}} a Clarified
expression. thou art.)

Blue Moon

I lay watching the blue moon rise

whispering in the candlelight,

by the windowsill aglow with the elements,

gazing past water glasses full of crystals and
moonbeams

"Illuminate my heart."

I did not beg to be broken again because, I knew it
to be accomplished….

This time, I asked to be remade.

All that I ever knew, or thought I was… no
more… no more….

…cycles of creation, cycles of destruction…

"Let me be transformed. Make all that I am,
yours…"

I repeated the names of God and breathed infinity,

relinquishing myself, as ever.

I felt my humanity slip away,

the colors came in, like a dragon's breath –

burning away the mundane to reveal hidden treasure, until sparks flew

Ah, heart… you stubborn, foolish thing…

gated with steely doors, bolted shut from life's pain but, at last…

they opened again.

It was a scene that came to my mind,

of great works, of a farm – of a man, clear as day, I've yet to meet

I felt at last, the great beast turn and open, revived… no small miracle.

I saw visions flush with happiness.

People working together, of life growing all around.

Risen from the ash (again and again and again),

I step forth, fresh from cosmic fire like a shiny new arrow.

Blue moonbeams running through my veins,

angels dancing round my bed.

"Guide me. I am ever thine."

Dr. Jones

Gentle words spoken in the afternoon,

I listen in the twilight of my work day,

alone in the office, and riveted.

Racing the red hawks on my way home,

your voice flew like campfire sparks, igniting my
mind.

Kindling rosy daydreams in my heart,

until I am made new, soft as a child ~

sweetened by wild blueberries,

warm under covers on snowy nights.

And when the wind howls like a banshee, pull me
in closer,

"You're safe. I've got you."

Northern lights above, we two, stretched out on the beach

under a pile of wool blankets….

watching the mighty green and gold brothers

drive their chariots across the canvas of night,

racing to hold the hands of a pink fire, dancer in the sky.

My eyes are open, glowing, with a new kind of vigor for life,

as the electricity of you goes racing through my veins.

Oh, happy kindness, gentle soul….

you have already conquered all resistance.

The weather is quickly changing, rolling her heat over

pulling her thick mane of clouds over your house,

fixing her blue-green eyes on you.

Do you feel her in the air?

Shaking with excitement, until your windows rattle?

And dripping with the condensation of her breath,

exhaling words like gifts from a land long forgotten, Dr. Jones

All from pictures drawn, of hot air balloons, of being next to you,

over Niagra Falls and the rarest natural beauties….

wandering the woods happily, as deer do.

<u>Incarnata</u>

I tried and failed. Where was the love in my heart?
Where raging passions once burned – was an
empty space, a quiet space, a void. My body
seemed to be crumbling around it… failing slowly.
A stiff back from nights in this mockery of a bed,
skin burnt in an instant from a morning in the new
spring desert sun despite every precaution, a
badly burned wrist seared from an unwise
combination of wine and late night cooking…. and
the weather vane of my life is spinning in all
directions, again…. yet, somehow there is peace.
Or is it more an alien neutrality of emotion with
nothing in my heart? Should I be terrified or
relieved? Fortunately, God has blessed me with
good work to lose myself in…

But, let me dream of all the qualities that would
inspire love…. sweetness, humor, laughter,
patience, strength of will, mind, body and spirit.
Determination, ingenuity, trustworthiness, loyalty,
wisdom, sensitivity, masculinity…. kisses that
make my head spin, arms eager to hold and keep
me. A body that is firm to touch, eyes that speak in
silence (so that I can read the past, present, and
future….) and a heart which beats with love
unafraid, unashamed – so that I will be brave and
feel the spirit of the earth rise within, begging for

all of life to exist and flourish, if for only this one, exact, moment.

Let it linger…..

Dancing until we are both breathless with laughter, in the garden gazebo will you find me alluring under the stringed white lights, enough to be overcome? Stop me. Press your lips to mine and like a song that tells a story of romance so true, felt by bards of years past and children future, kiss me. Kiss me with all that lives within you and I shall kiss you back, with the mysterious wellspring of my being. The goddess Aphrodite lives inside me and it is to her I pray – to fill me up with the secrets of beauty and love so that I am ever her vase. That is why the damp heat of you is my Eden, my reason for being. And when you kiss me by the ear, and my neck, my shoulder…. I become passiflora incarnata in the sun, transformed in a moment to be your wild breathless one.

I'm holding you in my heart. Come home to me, my hero…. my dream…. I shall be wandering by the sea shore, writing poems in the sand for you. Trailing my fingers across the damp surface of the beach, as if it were your body, strong and cast in sweet sweat, urgent for the soft curves of me against you. And when the tide comes in, your lips, which I shall kiss to remind me of the wetness of your mouth and the sparkle that never leaves your eyes. See me making garlands of shells? This is for the bower over our bed and with each one I string, I say, "Flower of passion be thine, pure of heart be mine, and in love may we be joined as one."

Aphrodite, do you hear?

Sun City

The rain clouds hanging low in the sky were a blessing…. a sight savored in the city of the sun. Sun eternal, sun through tall green palm trees, waxen and staunch, 40 feet high and blowing in the breeze. It was a morning of blood and pain, for me. Incredulous, bleeding animal. Senses heightened to the extreme; smell, sound, sight. I know what it is to be wild, primal, animalistic. My body knows it. It shows it, every month, at least once. I bought a broken wooden box, brand-new and a sack full of fleur-de-lis….. for a little project I'm working on. It may sound crazy if I say what it will be so I'll keep it to myself, for now. But, the box will be transformed for treasure, such treasures!

Afterwards, I drove to Sun City.

I realized the terrain reminded me of Ireland, even though southern California is the opposite of Ireland. But, the steep hills, the rolling hills, the rocky hills- now green with rain….. remind me of Ireland. That at least, I can live with. I stopped at Boston Billies in Sun City for a Rueben sandwich with fries to go. It was the real deal- the diner with maroon pleather upholstered booths, the patrons (all in their 80's), and the Rueben. Fucking great sandwich. Did I mention the place is run by Egyptians?

Then, my main event for Monday- a right on Grosse Point, a left on Allentown and I have time-warped into a dream from the 1950's where the lamps and couches are, just so. Everything is put in it's place. The air is calm and easy to breathe. The plush carpet is soft and thick and almost a deep shag and the paintings on the wall are done by Burgus… who I am talking too and towering over by about a foot and a tiny octogenarian named, Louise. We talk, we drink coffee, they teach me the secret signs of a secret society and I agree to be at their next meeting. We eat the cookies I brought and Burgus shows me his wood carvings, which are astonishing. Louise pulls her red Caddy out of the drive and I agree to practice the signs…. since I am not allowed to make notes in writing. I can't help noting that for how real everything is inside this precious ranch house…. it seems the more frail for it. The well loved porcelain statuettes, the glass globe lamps, the hand made doilies and afghans, the peach and cream satin upholstered mid-century couch….. the brown ducks in the wallpaper over there….. Sanka coffee and rock gardens instead of a lawn….. please never depart this earth. This flourescent light swathed plastic framed Diet Coke microchip airplane vodka tonic bombshell and warplane Walmart self-medicating world!! I need brown ducks in my wallpaper, damn it… never die.

(God, I'm homesick.) But, try as we might……
nothing was ever meant to last forever. And
nothing ever does and we all know it. It's what we
do with that knowledge that guides the path we
take….. some go straight and some go….

Shaking from three cups of coffee, driving in the
opposite direction on this stretch of now-known
Cali-Ireland with it's blessing of thick clouds,
thinking of alpacas and summer, thinking of
friendship and valleys, my grandmother- of the
actual probability of my being alone forever,
living high up on one of those big mountains way
up in the clouds, secret societies, and music….. of
what it all means, put together. And I thought of
you. (All of you.) I thought of what it all means, to
me…..

I am sooo far out…. in the rolling high green hills,
the rocky roads, the rolling valleys which will
burn with sun in 3 months…… burning with my
questions…. my quest. Burning with my
loneliness. I press these thoughts to my heart.
What shall be? I'll keep a sweet kiss in my mind
and joy behind my eyes instead of tears…. and
smile inside, for your sweet presence to be near
me. Because I know that in some backwards way, I
am actually in the midst of making all my dreams
come true. I am surrounded with the bounty of
every possibility, fruits of labor, ingenuity… my
love, the layers upon layers that line the coat of
my soul…. t'is a wonder to be sure, the colors gay,

I never tire of running the length of them, every one…. though I do long to love another, one other…. dear, sweet, and true.

Virtue

I tried to recall the feeling of virtuousness, purity

trying on different images to inspire the authentic recollection

the thing that it is – virtue.

I thought of Mickey Mouse and Mother Theresa

rescuers of abused dogs, brave children and firemen

It was only when I thought of Romeo and Juliet that I felt it

Pure love, true virtue.

Passionate, all-consuming love…

Virtue is the shadow of this kind of love, hurrying beneath its footsteps

Rushing to please, to surprise, to delight-

I love you like all of life loves the first days of Spring,

headstrong and full of songs for you.

I love you because wherever I look, I see you in someway

To me the world is a bounty from which I shall pull the very best

into my cakes and poems and dresses and lavish you with all.

The trees were talking to me, as the breeze blew.

They said, "I love you."

And I watched how their beauty poured out through their very bodies-

to be everything to me.

To be the air I breathe.

Dancing to be here, to be near….

Virtuous tree…

I wish to be as sweet and pure and good,

and love others as you do,

with all that you are.

For the sake of being present,

for the sake of giving,

for the sake of love…. sweet virtue.

That I would be this kind of Juliet,

this hopeful lover, ah me……

I watched the trees and knew innocence again.

Alien Alarm Clock

rum and unemployment

fast cars from the past guzzling gas like a pirate on
an island

with no place to go except the bottom of a bottle-

days run into nights and the nights seem to go on
for miles…

long black miles…

and then the aliens.

they made contact last night through my alarm
clock.

the light wavered and pulsed, moving like
glowing liquid

obscured and redefined (because time is not
numbers…)

it is one moment of focus.

riding the waves of light like… like….

a sea lion at night gliding over phosphorescent waters.

"What now?"

Peace, apprehension, run, stay, focus… just for a moment.

Hands pulling, kneading, pushing and grinding my body

Every muscle discovered, I wept in some places, my quiet pains found out

The lotion bottle, my feet touched by a stranger, (that's twice this week)

caressed…..

The masseur found midnight walks in bad shoes,

One car crash, a rather manic episode near a large dumpster

A backflip gone horribly wrong,

Hours of typing and hours of walking endlessly…..

they lived as memories unwanted in my very body.

She touched them until they cried again and then they were gone.

And now there is all of this lovely space.

Space in the morning, space in the night.

I have time on my hands again……. are you there?

My alarm clock wants to say something. "It's time."

It's time. It's time….. now what?

Carpet questions.

Coffee…..

And my attention. My Focus. My Awareness.

I am listening to the river.

I am listening to the lights streaming through my mind.

I am seeing green pastures and mountains, high above the water.

I am seeing great happiness. Triumph.

There are foggy areas I cannot see.

Possibilities which are too young and unsure…..

So I'll sit within my space today and dream.

I will dream up my moments, one by one.

Riding the river of my awareness…. until all is a rainbow and clear again.

Until all the colors are so bright,

I am half blind with ecstasy, hope, elation –

The quiet morning is singing in French and playing the guitar

but, I feel so far away……

as if I'm watching myself sit here in the corner of the room

like a shiny new balloon….

All the colors of the rainbow dancing dreams in my mind,

until all the rest is grey.

Ever After

It was the fight versus the ease….

The sun against the dark mean storm.

Tears to the winter tease… of steering clear or
nearing near (to you?)

But, what does it matter? The romance, the sex,
the excitement…..

When death of spirit is at hand?

Hacking away with micro-management, the hours
and the days

of control, of objectivity, hatred of women
disguised with lust for legs

Mother calls me a harlot,

and the plastic snowmen screech falsetto
Christmas carols….

in a McDonalds at midnight on Western Avenue

playing along with the lies and laziness of defunct men, drunk

jacking off to images with ill-intentions and no real direction

the lack of lovely hit me as I drove through the rain

sobbing for the lack… lack of it all.…

stark realizations in Korea-town

real as a Mexican in a black neighborhood

Mississippi soul food and Snooty Fox Motel

real as the crackhead with a backpack in only a nightgown

I am just a nothing

Just a figure passing through

Faces coming out of the rain

Morrison sang on the radio

When you're a stranger, people are strange

And he was right.

Black night in Los Angeles.

Windshield wipers, swish swash…. static on the line.

T'was a black heart…. so proud… like a tinsel float on the 4th of July

I had a fight within me… but…

It died drowning in paint and ruffles.

It died fighting against closed doors and egos.

It died struggling to be a light in a Hollywood alley.

(Like so many before?)

And the rain and the rules sought to quaff the embers….

Yet, I still live.

Yea…… I still breathe.

Revived and reminded by the upward spirals of a child's Disney flick…

portrait of the magic of Christmas…. and selflessness.

I am not a body.

I am a spirit.

I am love.

And by my very nature, indestructible.
Chaplin's Secret

Removing all my layers,

clothes to the floor,

1, the shirt

2, the skirt

3, the bra

…… and 4?

In Charlie Chaplin's bungalow

you ran your hands over me,

curvy like a tall Marilyn.

I moved against you, breast to hip,

like a river high with desire,

coursing strong and coming fast.

Your hands between my legs, moving like a sin…

and the kisses never stopped, nipples wet with
your lips…

Oh, you control my all….

By the Hollywood sign, for the first time, we saw

the full spectrum above. The skies shook and
moaned, incandescent

I, transformed with your touch, like clouds against
the sun.

The colors are so bright, this new inner sight
makes me wonder

have I been blind until now?

You are the torch which burns within me,

Flickering and steady with the bright teasing
tongue of Kundalini,

Yes, I swell at the thought,

shuddering with everything I am to be with you.

Bending beyond, even the confines of this body…

which, I will give you again and again.

Until the worlds outside fall into one another,

united and made sacred with the sounds of our
lovemaking.

I Am Touching You

Are you touching me?

I can see you.

Can you see me?

You do. I know it. Like no other, so clearly.

Facing you after so much has passed between....

time, lives, bottles, and open highways.....

Eyes blink. I face you and my destiny.

And I twirl my hair nervously

not knowing what I say.

Words? You smile again and my heart races.

(coloring me pink and pinker in all places)

I squirm and squeal like a young girl,

unable to stop myself from blushing louder.

You are so calm…. so serene…. so….

You are like another language

And I….. am captured by some invisible hold

Curious and unsure of what to do with you

My heat rises and I become some kind of…

defenseless animal- removed from every part of my mind.

You watch and know and smile with delight,

my twirling hair, my pink cheeks, my crisscrossing legs, and long fingers…

Fidgeting with my mouth as I get more and more nervous

Drinking wine to calm myself and growing more irrational

What are these words? I hardly know them.

Who is this fidgeting body, soaring inside,

like a fighter jet spinning out of control.

All I see is you.

Your dark eyes, your strong kind face... so handsome.

I could paint you right now.

It would be the most attractive painting....

I would use warm tones like oak and redwood

Gold for the light.... all the light around you....

gold breasted nymphs leaning in for a caress...

such is the light around you.

Seeking out all the parts of you that rest in the shadows.

What are those shadows to you?

Nothing, everything.....

I am touching you. Are you touching me?

)))))))))))))))::x::(((((((((((((((

Orange sun shineth like an autumn star,

….down upon me….

lingering on the lip of your horizon,

breathing in and out your kisses-

Holy Son, you're the one, for me.

Radiance in waves of hot, sure sex.

Embracing me 'round, holding and
emboldening….

You are the brilliant bright heart, I seek

was searching for……. so sure… more than ever I
hoped for

What most perfect fate, that we now meet.

In tea houses and bedrooms, in the eternity of my
mind

you are with me always,

will you be my Valentine?

Smiling the way you do, an easy king

a wealth of golden happiness in the rays of your joy…

Amber skies over hazy gold fields,

the wildflowers and red leaves, the moon, the violet stars

Lead me to the place, where only breath lives

Your hands on my skin, where only hearts beat

My weight upon your body like a pillar and the splendor of Heaven

coursing through our veins like red lightening,

increasing with every second, pressing next to you.

Kissing and moving ever towards,

like a lost star caught in the gravity of your love, your heat

So pull me close….. I am high in your orbit

moving around and around and around…..

covering you with the sweetest of affection, completely…

Touch me with your hands…..

I can feel you inside.

Be now everywhere to me.

Rin.

Lulu, you were the Russian grey voodoo.   A
BEAUTY.

with yellow eyes

and beating heart

kept my best friend abreast

through Las Vegas

and Maryland…. new marriage, the cat that she
loves best

….. Erin, sweet friend, I love you

these are the things we must do sometimes

the hardest, most horriblest things……

Erin, by the bridge. Erin with the mask I made you
wear

10 years ago by the Loch Raven Resevoir….

Erin. These things sometimes must be.

My sweet friend. My darling…. and her darling….
LuLu.

Sweet, soul. Soar tonight in the stars.

Be the comet that you are.

Sweet senorita.

Peace will reign.

Sweet peace and blessings to the spirit of Lulu,
your soft companion.

Be as things all must be…..

Sweet honey…

Soul like clouds, soft as milk

Night like my most favorite song,

I swear she is aloft, my sweet

watching down over you, hon

………. Erin? What can I do?

99#2y)#)HD+Dksa

culdesac of whistles and white trucks
of Hot Wheels and baseball, everyday
the chiuaua, Marley competes with the stray cat
large and orange, so I call her Pumpkin
I wear earplugs for my afternoon naps
and read of a woman and her bees 'round 6
I go week in and week out
no touch, no contact
with anything of meaning, outside
my books
and a bottle of wine
or the hard stream of a shower
or the salty strong wave of the sea
only lately have I begun working
in the corporate structure of technology
plugged into the mainframe
analyzing the data
where the men in white suits
shuffle to make microchips
using hot gas and acids
burning the lines of progress
into the future of our minds
our very day to day
twittering and tittering our lives away
talking faster, saying less

In India, they say this isn't happiness
In Africa, they say this is no kind of progress
In Australia…. they agree, that only music
sweet soul music, is the kind of story
we can tell
from heart, with hands
dancing, eyes to hips, laughing from ear to ear
is what, (no tears), we may love life with
when there is no one to talk to
no one to touch
and the noise is all around
like the beehive buzzzzzz
sing a song, dance the ragtime
and even in the desert….
where the lizards lie
and the crows fly black against the sunny
sunny, sunny sky
you will never be alone.

California Wildfires

8 months and 4 states later, I find myself in California
pelted by an all-pervasive sun,
surrounded by sentient palms, alien in form
in the distance, the royal ocean beckons, a blue Queen
crashing into my consciousness with the tides of her turning
I watch the gulls and pelicans lift and fall,
in between the breakers, fishing for silvery answers to an instinct
It is what perhaps, led me here, to this wandering,
traipsing from coast to coast on a diet of adrenaline and dreams
seeking some kind of salvation
Fishing for the restored bounty of my soul,
I threw my line out into the void, time after time, turning up clues
Oh, there have been ugly nights…
and incandescent discoveries aplenty,
as I have turned the page on each day,
trying to escape my thoughts of you.
It is with some dark amusement,
now reflecting on the past three years I have spent in devotion

anguished and elated on the rocky road of our love,
at last proved to be… fragile as a sickly child,
choked on the poisoned hook of idle gossip from my foremost enemy.
At long last, I can give up the ghost of my screaming madness
At long last, my vigil is abolished by this final banal excuse
pointing, yet again, to what I blind fool I have been…
I'll raise my voice alongside these burning mountains,
consumed by bright flames, stretching across the sky
And burn the memory of my headstrong passion until the sky is draped in black smoke
howling like a rabid wolf,
my laughter will ring out for the waste of it all
HAHAA!!!! it was all such a glorified waste, all such a lie….
and this clarity will consume the foolhardy mountain
which, was steadfast as my love, patient and willing to be
always, your resting place, your highest peak
but, kneel now in humility, black faced and charred.
Stripped of life. Reduced to wasteland.
This journey is at last, complete and I am no longer steadfast
no longer the mount, unmoved by travesty,

no more the prevailing testament of undying love.
At least not for you.
I shall be as the wind, body and soul
searching on wings, for the fragments of my heart
which, I sent out in letters and poetry, all
addressed to…
I shall rest only in the arms of God at night
and walk the holy Earth from end to end,
murmuring prayers for my soul's wholeness
Prayers of forgiveness and mercy,
for something new to love,
I will pray until my heart is full again.
For now it is empty, forsaken, as ever……
Besieged by the triviality you claim excuses your
silence….
proffered as a beggar's meager crumbs,
oh, I have feasted on these rotted morsels for so
long…
My enemy sought to part us and now
I cannot help but, to laugh….
I see how all the pain I have known and endured,
was caused by my own hand,
by giving more and accepting less.
All hail, the dark comedian!
He comes smiling with pointed teeth.
And I am dancing with him, hand in hand.
For your claims are empty, your love a dime store
postcard never sent
And amidst the California wildfires, I am in my
element-
at last freed from the prison of my illusion.

And I walk away laughing from the wreckage of it all.

Tennessee

Hot Tennessee, how you defy and capture me
between sheets sheer with sweat
in a bedroom of pale sky… and grassy green
Nighttime creeksong in the water under moonsky
reflecting 8 bare legs, wading in the cosmos-
Infinite woman, sanctify us.
I am the believer and the peacemaker,
the dreamer and the dream,
I am a child of the wild woods,
dancing with three sisters in a midnight brooke.
In the dirt road and the clay, where we dig along
on our private agendas and problems.
I find counsel in the weeds and unwanted timber
and in the sweat of our backs-
moving in unison, an answer to the truest prayer I
ever knew
running through the trees at night, alongside and
behind you.
You are my light and my new lantern,
following you around is all I have time for
anymore,
learning your little ways.
On the lawn, lounging on an oriental carpet
writing about people swinging over there-
here, we are the children of Sonnenshein
imbibing Bob Dylan and orange blossom honey
goat's milk soap scented with Eastern Evergreen
white trucks rumble by

as the white haired woman carrying a strawberry
dipped in wet chocolate crosses the lawn
oh my, what a fine June Saturday!
Motorcycles ride by the school grounds growing
clovers
after ice coffee and yard saleing
now its all over for me, young strong Tennessee….
you are a dangerous kisser,
got a certain swank in your swagger
and you sure look damn fine to me.
I'll be your lady, your lover, your friend
loving you in fields lit with Queen Anne's Lace
moonlit meadows move like the sea where the
dark horses graze
Come wrap your arms around my waist and turn
me round again…

Tremble

Tremble light on the water, slowly riding by
Watching from the mossy banks, soft and still I…
hear the deer, delicate, stepping through the
leaves
and smile in surprise at the amber butterflies on
the breeze

Tremble bright, sweet love… as dew upon the
web
fall upon the clay of me and be the stream where I
am the stream bed
Drifting far, out to where there is no fear
until return becomes a paradox, for all roads lead
to here

Tremble moon, silver spell caster high above
Spill yourself into my wine and let me know a
night of love
where the ants go marching one by one
and the lightening strikes like liquid sun…

Tremble heart, with all I've yet to know…
wake me from this endless dream, deep in sleepy
hallow
lead me across open fields, where the flowers are
high and wild

take me to sandy shores where I can dream like a
child

Tremble here, how I shall tremble near
his beating heart where my beating heart
make love bold as summer days

Young blood, old wisdom; walk awhile-
here in the hold of nature's road
where the rising sun, sets my soul ablaze.

Spring Alchelmy

Warm as a child, the day wraps itself around me
Soft, sea-blue skies move as waves and
Fleets of cloud ships led by billowing sails white,
high above
the parade where crowds of newly minted leaves
upon the trees
move in jubilee, casting vestiges of their former
selves,
in pink and white petals, tossed
bouquets of silken delicacy, fluttering to the
earth…
In gales of innocent beauty….
I have seen no greater celebration.
As I was walking in this reverie,
a young salamander caught my eye,
fire red, was he-
bringing the mark of transformation across my
path,
(and alchemized by the Green Lion)
I wept upon the white stone as he slipped away,
the quickening spirit harkens to the fire of
enlightenment

the realization of which, electrifies
causing stillness to whirl like a child's
kaleidoscope.
My soul speaks to me in tongues,
as the green cicadas sing in shrill multitudes;
many yet, one.
So, too, do the eyes of peacock fans, promenading
across the lawn
speak of life's endless possibilities,
painted in every color of the day
though these same spectrums
reflect in the hot glisten of the raven's black
Is there really such a creature as evil?
I muse the secrets of the universe by the dogwood
tree
where I recline in wonder upon my back.
Trembling in joy, as much as awe
for spring's quick pace and terrible
thunderstorms,
heat lightening followed by burst of sudden sun,
gentle rains on the heels of wind with such a
fury….
Yea, there never was a storm or a season of more
loveliness.
Rainbows are made of her tears and life of her
raptures.
Overcome, my being empties its pockets
and stands ready for motion, ask of me,
anything….
For my heart is swelling with the heady season of
eternal youth.

Ever smiling , eager for the taste of romance's first
kiss,
My spirit new as the pink in each cherry blossom's
pretty face,
Oh, brave and tender Love! I shall always be thy
resting place!

::::::))))))))))nakedlaundry(((((((((::::::

overcast afternoon, promising rain
the breeze toys with new blooms
ever so flirtatiously, with a come hither tickle
under their chins.
almost envious, I watch with some unspoken wish
unclear even to myself, until the laundry blew my
way
where I was hanging the clothes along the line
it was the ghost of a caress long forgotten…
oh, the stirring of my soul!
no longer under the fold of those pleasures and
pains
of memory, though there are many to choose…
Clean as the wet clothes dripping onto my bare
feet
my heart too, is on the wind, heading in
unexpected directions
a way revealing itself to me in tiny glimpses
of dreams and flights of fancy, crows and
midnights
and the fox I saw thrice!
I know he saw me too, from the road where I was
passing,

I spied his bushy red tail and fine nose and ears,
heading into the woody dark… to me he says,
"Be cunning, my pet! Tread with care in your
wilderness!"
And the rain is coming now to soak the seeds I
have planted,
hear that thunder? That's love, baby. Love for
my…
moonflowers and poppies…
sunflowers….morning glories….
I spoke to each one as I patted them into the earth.
'you are my love, grow for me my love!'
'you are my beauty, grow for me my beauty.'
'you are my fortune, grow for me good fortune.'
(there are seeds named for forgiveness,
compassion,
and clarity, too…)
I watered them on the full moon whispering,
Shanti, shanti, shanti…..
With the storm coming, I can think more clearly,
when the sky is not quite dark but, not quite light
either…
moving everywhere at once, fast enough to make
you spin
and the trees go dancing in excitement, those very
tall trees….
still skeletal against the sky, for spring has only
just begun her magic.
The wind casts the dead leaves of winter,
across the mossy lawn like a big broom.
I, too, feel that the time has come, to be moving
on….

How did 3 months go by? I am waking from a
long slumber…
A sleep so deep, I forgot who I was before…
And now I am someone who dances once more in
the kitchen,
No agenda or mission… I just am.
I exist, lifted by my gratitude,
for having lived it through this far.
But, now where to? Now I must decide… where
to?

Countryside

Miles of countryside, spring to life on daylight savings.
80 degrees under a sunny haze by the river,
my dog and I wandered where the water rushed impatient
emboldened by yesterday's melted snow, the daffodils bloom
new in yellow and white at the feet of 100 year old trees
strong and gnarled with the ages of America,
where we are the daffodils.
Temperate visitors trumpeting our brief but, loud existence
This morning, at a 50's diner for breakfast,
I sat across the table from my mother
sipping coffee out of heavy ceramic mugs an inch thick
and ice water from small brown glasses.
I felt my love renewed, as she laughed at her own story
it was if I was seeing again her for the first time,
this beautiful woman with sunshine in her smile.

I feel transformed by rest. My vision and judgment are reborn,
for the countryside is a new found luxury of which I will never tire,
Acres of open land containing stories of lives lived in cabins and farmhouses
both opulent and meager,
with gardens and greenhouses, ponds and barns strong workhorses and fine riding horses, long necked llamas,
and woolly sheep outnumbered by the herds of mild cattle
who dot the green fields in black, red, and white.
I felt the space, I feel the space. How good it is….
this permission to breathe easy.
Inhaling peace and clean air deeper than you ever dared breathe
…in Manhattan.
Here, where every store is an hour away
and your nearest neighbor is a 30 minute walk.
In such a place, all that seemed important before, has no meaning or cause to exist.
Your thoughts pertain to the number of fingers on one hand….
Family, friends, nature, your craft or art-
and the elegance of your communion with each of them.
This is the fabric of life, void of the plastic spangles
and drive thru junk food of the new media
corrupt civilization now a sinking ship, watch the dollars drop

as litter to the floor, just like before.
The living world of nature is our cradle,
come home children.
It is night now and outside the inky sky
is lit with lunar rainbows, circular, pastel and
iridescent.
Full moon rising through the heated clouds
and the breeze moves the trees to creaking
carrying the newborn crickets' happy symphony
along with the comical tenor of bullfrogs,
not to be ignored-
through the screen window.
Their music means life and the warm night speaks
of love
through the rushing rivers and the growing
wildflowers
in the thunder of a hundred pony hooves,
kicking their heels in the heat along the coast,
which brought
the casting of fishing lines from little boats
holding fathers and daughters, brothers and
sisters,
sons, wives, husbands,
old friends and young friends calling to the
children on the shore
who are splashing each other at the water's edge
which makes the old people laugh
who are picnicking together at the lake….
How love fills this great space.
Oh, the city is like a bad dream I had a lifetime
ago…

and my heart is full of peace and quiet, out here in the country.

Meditation on Silence

Friend of silence. Quiet is my heart in the peace of silence. In stillness, I rest safe and warm as the fieldmouse in her mossy bed. Gone is the chatter of busy minds and street traffic. Gone irreverence, plucky wit, crude humor. Gone comedic folk and lesbian rap duos, white trash metal, and reincarnated psych reverb. Gone Byronic bleeding hearts and blackened eyes. Gone bar banter and mindless talk radio. Gone speeches of politic and corporate memos repeating "war and recession". Gone the cry of a world in peril, the echoes of apathy, the battle calls of hopeful martyrs, the starving children of Africa, the beaten, the bruised, the wise and the confused. Hush, all. The silence washes you away. Your rude cacophony is swallowed at the mouth of the well which holds the waters of all creation. All that you are is liquified by the sweet ripple upon the surface of the zero point. The beginning and the end. The silence before the sound. The dark stillness before the light of life's to and fro.

My meditation of silence cleanses, soft and pervasive as steam. White clouds of it thicken the air with a neutral presence. A silent being, devoid of character or opinion. Isness. Where thoughts exist in an infinite space, big enough to wear themselves out. Vast and whole enough to strip the trappings of words and actions down to their nakedness. My mind is clean of all that was now wise with all that is. I am the silence. I am the stillness. In the womb of creation, I am the consciousness meditating quietly. Surrendering my actions, I become aware of true greatness.

A Drop of Sweat

Is not all of creation reflected within a drop of
sweat?
Here, at your mouth…
lips red with kissing, breath exhaled in quick
gusts,
your body dripping
with the giving of yourself to me.
And like the Earth who lays beneath,
I turn with your pinching and slapping,
I shudder, as the quake, which sank the great cities
for when you touch, I erupt in beautiful violence,
screaming yes yes and please please
Slowly in the aftermath…
I stroke you trembling
though the rest is throbbing,
growing hotter than before
and to let you know I am nibbling
at your ear… seducing you slowly
tracing circles from there to there
because my body is aching and awaking
with visions of you and me and me and you…
down on the bedroom floor.

Can there be another lover for me?
I move against you and you look as none I've ever
seen.
Your words spoken in the heat of lovemaking say,
"You are so beautiful. I can't believe how good
you feel."
Is this real? I can hardly believe, how risque'.....
how surreal….
I am light as air, with your hands right there
and in our cries I hear the tides crash upon the
shores of divinity.
Your appetite aroused,
between my legs as they spread and go up and
down
My lips suck, my hands caress
eyes look up with hungriness
but, I cannot outlast your strength
You are the sun
…and I am a Georgia highway, soaked in summer
rain
hot and wet, you go the length
until at last we toast with the last few sips of warm
champagne
Sink here, next to me. Breathe here, next to me.
Hearts beating, excitedly. Spines tingling,
delightedly.
Two bodies as one and the veil parts, we float
above our bed
disembodied ecstasy our spirits high we race the
stars
led through the Milky Way far past our planet of
blue-

There we are, just me and you.

888((O))888

Wash me clean of the cold sorrow of my former life, love…. you are the sacred rain, relentlessly pouring yourself forth to seek me out. Here is where I am found. Here I am the golden meadow, seed me with your fulfillment and wander the seasons of my soul. Take in the full measure of my gaze and I yours. See here, liquid pools of naked innocence deep with the expression of joy, unclouded by the burden of secrets no longer kept. See there, the simmering desire to consumate my fair body with every pleasure known between us. The uncertainty of the night exists no longer…. kiss me, love. Undo my complications with each opening button on my dress. Make me simple again. In the divine dawn, I awake with the sway of my hips, mid-slumber. Press me with your sweet motivations and take me with your lips. Under you, smooth as milk and sweet as pale roses, I embrace every part of you. I taste the completion of our bodies, one to the other, as wild honey warmed with the sun of enjoyment. You transform me with your affections until I am willing to bear fruit and gift you with a bounty for centuries to come. Moon waxing, white hot as

Heaven's gate, luminous and impetrenable by the wicked but, flood me with your loving presence and let me be opened and released as never before. In the surge of your power shall I sing such notes of cosmic rapture that the stars will burst overhead with cherubim ecstasy. Come, take my hands. Whisper to me the words I must hear. The nightengale serenades and the silver aspens sway gently outside our window. Do you hear the day breaking on utopia? It sounds like the orgasmic cry of angels, moving in cosmic harmony. An acapella of sexual union resounding from the crumbling walls of ancient lore to the newly born comet shooting over our Eden. You are the key to grace and I am the gate of infinity. Turn in me the joy of your heart and let our combined love unleash a new age of heaven on earth. For here is the wellspring of all existence. Drink with me from the chalice of pure love and in every sip will we imbibe peace, such sweet peace….. that the hallows of our fine house will shake with the laughter of friends and good company, that our plates will be filled with the life of food that is pure and abundant without slaughter or slight, that our work will be plenty and honest, and our amusements many as the wild flowers which hail the health and sanctity of our planet. Usher in with me, The Age of Harmony. Oh, love… my true hero…. sanctify my heart and take me for yours. I forsake all that was the battlefield of my former self and no longer wrestle with the ghosts of my loneliness, my separateness. I offer you my wholeness, my completeness. I offer you infinite pleasure and eternal love. I offer you my humility and my loyalty. I offer you my laughter and joy. I offer you peace and wisdom…. oh, Love…. let it be.

IIIIIIIIIIIIIIIIII

Day half lit and pale
streaming weakly into the attic room
where layer, after layer, after layer….
I make my bed thick with memories of you.
It was only for a moment, brief…
as a flutter of the dusty moth upon the sill,
as the frozen wind tosses a long-dead leaf,
broken in the groans of yonder trees gone frail…
stripped bare by Winter and lit by Moon.
The radiance of night now surpasses that of day,
the bejeweled jet sky bends to kiss a barren earth.
When all of life is absent and sunlight yields to
starlit rays-
When the snow fox dances, t'is then I know my
birth.
My wintered soul rejoices in the silent solace,
blanketed in white, the earth begins again…
with every wish that joy surpass the evils which
may befall us
It is the season of alpha and omega; all beginnings
and every end.
And in the shortness of the day, by the lengths of
night

Whether I sit by fire burning,
or stride across vast fields of snow,
I banish the unrequited phantoms of my yearning,
As wood to fire and black to crow.
Extinguished are the dreams, that I'd be yours or you'd be mine..
For every present possibility exists, the sacred seed
Now watered and sown in the field of space and time.
Oh, I'll be happy, Love… so happy I'll soar high above
Happy as a newborn babe, happy as a morning dove…
I am free my Love…. free as I can be my Love….
No more sorrow, only joy and cheer-
Every second, every hour; year after year after year, my Love….

.sugarsnow.

Frost wind bites and your eyes gleam bright,
illumined by a noble mind

Laughter rings from tree to tree
'neath this canopy of Earth's divine

Come taste me here by the maple tree,
sugar snow now I know what love is…

Frozen hands find me warm and squirming under
their chill,
be still!

So go… no come… in the winter woods…
oh, shall I know what love is?

Race yonder ruddy sun falling fast
we chase the horizon and when you ask,

"My sweet girl can this last?"
I reply, "The day cannot but my love will."

…in the winter woods. on the sugared snow. by
the maple trees…

as the sun sets gold in woods
enchanted with sighs lifted by a frozen breeze…

Soft and tender in the twilight
take me here as I breathe, "Now I know what love
is."

<u>.orientmountains.</u>

It was in sleep, deep as the sound of a timeless chant, droned in divine vibration across Orient mountains: that was the plane in which we met again. In the gray muggy morning, I can only recall elements, the details have been washed by the new rain of a new day, but those thoughts that longed for expression now know freedom for when I awoke, your smile still lingered in my mind. We walk through a cynical world, spiked with bitter sarcasm against that which brings any hope to a population besieged by a souless existence- generations gone dark and dormant through the constant feed of a throwaway society reared on the commercialism of pop culture. Cartoons, consumerism, superficialized sex, and violence… the addiction of reality television that is anything but real. Orphans, all of us- set loose from the start to find our own way in a world shaped by power struggles and psychological neoteny. Where else can truth be seen, as easily as in the realm of dreams?

In the balm of life, that honey left in the wake of circumstance which has ripped away the veil, I breathe out a word of grateful recognition to that which rushes in, hand-in-hand with Truth. My mind and heart clear after yet another storm, I see the splendor of our world with eyes of a hawk soaring high above. What poetry stirs my heart? Today, in the summer rain, I smiled happy for the early hour which found me drenched alive, awake to the tremulous field always awaiting our discovery. Our sorrows and tragedies serve us in rousing the sleeping parts of ourselves. In them, we discover our greatest potential. The onslaught of distractions melt away and it is then that we realize our thoughts and feelings shape our world as real as buildings shape city skylines.

Wake lucid to the light hovering in the air all around us. The electric fabric from which we are all a part responds to pulse of thought, pulse of emotion as material shaped by a tailor. Whose clothes do you wear? By night I weave my world brilliant in awareness. By day, my awareness falls prey to the sounds and sights of a conglomerate reality and in its cacophony, cognizance is blurred. Power in remaining steadfast in the truth that we are more than just a physical body. We are the alchemists of our world. In the quiet of my morning, I have remembered to tell you how much I love you. Nothing that has passed between us, before or after, will ever make me forget that truth. Let us go forth, inseparable in Spirit, brilliant in Thought, and boundless in Love. For in this way, we become the awakened Dreamers of the Dream.

.atonement.

In the quiet repose of distant window gazing to where I was once invited

I feel a little stabbing at my heart,
a choking sob stopped by stubborn refusal

To be hurt by you or your judgment of me
because after all, it is I who left

Following the freewheeling ways of my own heart
I left you standing

Forsaken and slack-armed
on an empty highway of choosing

My dear, you never were good at walking alone

and though I sometimes wish to be with you

I relish in the bliss of my self atonement.

<u>.cigarette.</u>

cigarette.
in my mouth.
lungs.
breathing
out into the dark alley
leaning over my broken balcony
where i
look out at
such newly
lost
dreams
of love…

<u>Canary Islands</u>

Under an African sun I lay hypnotized in the
dunes…
by the tangerine sky kissing my cradle of sand,
where the camels lope and a Spanish parrot flies
o'er head…
watching my face grow damp with the heat of my
heart's own breath…
Beating hard to be held by you.
Now hear a symphony hum along with my
blood's hot race
Sing you a song from the otherside…
Poetry pouring like a king's tonique into my
ears…
I am consumed by riptide, a strong rift in the wake
of winter…
My little ship teeters, departing now from the
frozen beach
To find you riding the third wave where the
dolphins curve their backs.
I am spinning….around and around in cycles of
storm, of sea, of me-
of we.

Press me into the Earth until I've flowered here..
Come the garden grows wild and the night
jasmine sweats in anticipation.
Delay no further.. for we are shedding skins like a
garter snake…
Draw the line where the lily grows before the lily
goes…
Past the forest's edge beyond the hazy field
brimming with deer…
Past the skyscraper's gleaming like stars through
the morning city fog..
Past remote hopes and dreams, secret obsessions
and hatreds…
To the space where there is naught else but
space…
Paint me a picture of…
Above as below. Below as above.
Show me the holy center in this circle of love.

only.lonely.traffic

It is here in this white walled room standing high
by the freeway near the city skyline
that I lay in feathered longing, aching
to be touched by soft lips
now during dusky twilight
that I want your hands in my hair
pulling, pushing your body into mine
ankles, wrists bound by your clasp
open mouth catches falling sweat
but, no moans fill the air…
…only lonely traffic.

.Nocturna.

Nocturnal solitude
so seems an eternal quiet
in the comfort of dawn's prelude
Tonight my blood is thick
and the slur of time unravels
its mystery in veils
For comfort smoothes the temper
to a calm lapping of thought
Yea, for naught, the daily torrent
of chatter unheard by ears
plagues me in my sleep
Wrested from sleep the worry wakes me
panic flirting with my emotions
my loyalty tears me apart
and I ask myself to divide
and stay whole at once
Shambled temples are my virtues
But in the night of nights
I rest with one thought, you.

.rush over me.

rush over me as the breeze,
warm and wild through the curtain, he comes.

like an old friend and my only company,
drunk on sunlight spinning faster than country
circus lights
oh, how my mind runs…

but, listen listen! i am ready so hold me steady
with both your hands around my hips.

now hear me unleash the harlot, the tigress, the
temptress
when you press against me with your lips.

move me lover and hear me moan, like no other
when you take me to that heaven that i call home.

rush in, rush out- eyes aflutter, mouth open wide.

oh, holy gate! come to unlock the mysteries
that await between my thighs…

the sweat beads upon your brow,
runs in rivulets down your chest….

clutch of hands in hair and around my neck
bow me back as an instrument

play me lover, like a sonata-
until i sing and every string begins to shake…

take me until we can no longer
and then one more time until i break.

touch me like the lightening.

move me like the thunder.

come to me like a storm at sea,
be the tidal wave to take me under…

brave like the sun and solemn as the moon,

in the eve between garden leaves, sown of earth-

I'll be yours- yes, yours… one of these summer
afternoons….

.dragon of time.

dragon of time, lacing the sky with circular promises, i see your fire on the horizon. hawk wings fly and i spy the golden arrow darting.

racing towards you reckless with the strength of one thousand wild horses, i kick the past while running to my future.

palace of lace i stop myself in your webs. come find me now, in the center, contemplating in silence.

there is here. here is there. where am i? where am i? i am all places at once. name me into existence.

the wheels turn faster in the sky so i'll watch my hypnotic clock… faster faster! but, no… go slow…..

raised up, electrified by cosmic sexuality… She, Divine sent her dark Lover to my bed… together they annointed every inch.

bestowed gifts of radiant kiss, silk to touch, and drenched in lust… He covered me in his cloak. It flashes gold and red to the unseen eye.

what power is this and why? dragon of time… are you mine? am i Her daughter now? where have i gone? name me (human).

watch for me at sunset… my nature has become a beacon yet now I have lost sight of my own compass. spin the dial or spin the bottle. just kiss me.

your ethereal marionette… it's just a matter of time before I take back the strings.

Eros, what have you in store tonight?

.kissmetouchme.

Against the slur of soft city sounds,
on the warm hush of a summer night,
do I lay here wired and weary
and wrapped in my thoughts of you….
oh, how the tide goes out for you and I…
on the wake of my incurable temper.
Fast and wicked, easy to bruise,
I'm easy to lose and too quick to fight.
But you are deep in me, my love-
nothing left to prove…
So here I am again, heart ablaze,
heady gaze,
eyes burning bright as cinders.
Won't you soothe me with your hands
and stroke me 'til I am quiet?
I'll kiss your face and every place
while you gently pet and hold my hair…
There is nothing you can ask that I'll refuse,
so c'mon and try it.

Whisper, "kissmefuckmesuckmeandnowlet me touch
you everywhere."
Because you and I, what some may only dare dream,
we've been through it.
And no one loves me quite like you do….
And I don't trust anyone quite as I trust you….
And you, my love, you…
possess the only arms I want to run into.

liquid hysteria poured into mouth stirred through ears, exodus through tears. was the coldness or the silence more liberating than devastating? questions to be answered now free from the quiet pacing of sanity, back again to thrashing from the tree of my mind's shaking branches. i will close the book on you under sweat soaked sheets and when next we meet, eyes filled with so many words unsaid my thoughts will take me back to my bed where i have been loved and left. men play a cruel game. oh, these wicked hooks of attachments; i chose to lose you for the brace of Spring wind in my hair. eyes pressed closed against mountain meadow rain yes, some kind of happiness has sprung from your gifts of despair, some kind of life is lived is living is giving to someone somewhere…

.forsaken.

Thrown to the street at 3am with the freeze of bitter words, despite the roaming of hot hands. Quelle surprise the tears ran like rivers for days. How fitting for have I not ever poured myself out to you in every way? In love. In thought. In gifts and time. And favour upon favour, your eternal praise upon my lips and your forgotten fortune in my pocket I came bearing all across the night alone, through the dark….. Cast out and unjustly condemned. Again. Through carelessness you begin in punishing yourself but, end by punishing me. Blind to your device, you show me the truth in your rare cruelty. And there is always another face to replace mine. You have proved me expendable for the last time. So take your reward now in the absence of my love. The liquid bounty of my heart has stopped short in your shadow… for I finally realize, in your eyes, I am nothing but a way to pass the hours. Broken, my enduring delusions of love are at last dispelled. Let us both love the freedom of truth revealed. I am your fool, no more.

breathe you in...

breathe you in, down to my toes
i take you in until you are a part of me,
fill every cell of my being with your essence-
saturate every inch of me with your divine
attention, Love.
alchemized: i am more than who i was, a solitary
fragment,
a reflection of sky
for you make me brave with your
kissing.me.electrified with delight!!
in your arms i am a star afire alive but, hold on
hold on….
oh, you are so strong….

((0))

Phantom flower in the sky I lay under drenched in you, showered by your adoring gaze I am your rapturous butterfly. Watch as I draw close to your face in kisses, hot with fervent devotion….

Your radiance now quietly wild it captivates me and I am yours… yours…. oh, the tendrils of the Earth brush me to shivers passing through the garden in midnight rapture… searching only to be found by you, my love…. I spread my wings in your discovery… search me out for I am twirling esctatic…by these vibrations, tremored trails cast by fingertips softly on your face… down your neck to where the thunder lives calling me in heavy beats, like a stampede of horses running down the plains of your torso I go.. I go… to the valley of your stomach and down down below, down onto my knees in revelry for what you are about to do when I do what I do because every inch of me was made to make you feel Divine.

To be Divine.
To seetouchtasteandbe Divine.

Be my temple tonight…